A GUIDE TO REGLUEING and BASIC FURNITURE REPAIR

By

Cindy Haas

Foreword

Cindy Haas began her woodworking career in 1984 in a small shop owned by her and her husband. Over the years she has expanded her knowledge of the trade to include not only repairs, but designing and building her own cabinets and furniture. Cindy's knowledge also includes all types of finishes, veneering, laminates, hand caning, seat weaving and upholstery.

Cindy loves antiques and other beautifully designed furniture and by repairing them she helps to preserve the craftsmanship that defines the pride of our past. In this text she shares with you some of her best techniques to repair valued pieces. By giving you step by step instructions and pictures to accompany them, she hopes you will find them helpful and useful as you undertake your own project.

INDEX

CHAPTER 1- Supply list and Safety

- Rubber Mallet or a padded club

- WOOD GLUE, not white craft glue, hot glue or epoxies

- Masking tape and a marker pen

- 80, 150, 220 grit sanding papers and a wood file

- Drill and drill bits (3/8, 5/16, 7/16 and 1/2 are the most commonly needed)

- Clamps (C-type, pipe; depends on the piece to be repaired)

- Safety goggles and dust mask

- Paper towels

- Pliers, screw drivers, chisels, Dremel tool and attachments, ice pick or awl, and tooth picks

- Replacement dowels for broken dowels

- White Vinegar

Items above can be obtained at your local home improvement store.

You will also need a flat work surface that's clean and at a comfortable height.

SAFETY FIRST AND FOREMOST, especially with power tools. Read any and all operation manuals for the power tools. Wear safety goggles, dust mask and even a shop apron is a good idea. Take care that all loose clothing and hair is tied securely back out of the area. If you are tired or distracted don't work on your project, that is when mistakes are made and people get hurt.

Never assume that because a job looks easy, things can't go wrong, always go through the process mentally step by step.

CHAPTER 2 - Labeling and Disassembly

Figure 1 Labeling all parts, legs, rails, stretchers, & glue blocks

To begin, study the object you are regluing, and if any pieces are unattached, dry fit them back into place. Label all parts using the masking tape and marker. (Fig. 1) Make sure that when labeling parts you note the order from top to bottom and front to back. For example, note the order of rungs or stretchers on the chair in Figure 1. Often they are different lengths. You will find it beneficial to take pictures. Be sure to note angles and basic construction of the piece. Look for any nails or screws holding parts together at this time and remove them. Look for broken dowels and have replacements on hand before beginning. If working on case goods, the back may need to come off at this time to access interior supports. After labeling and familiarizing yourself with the piece, you can then begin to knock it apart, using the mallet or padded club. A gentle tapping is recommended; although, it can take a hard knock to take furniture apart. If a joint is tight and not yielding, I recommend leaving it alone, unless you actually can feel movement. If too much force is applied you can split the wood and break dowels. If a piece is loose, but not coming apart, clamp it tight to the work area and wiggle it while pulling on it. Sometimes a rotating circular motion works well for chair rungs, or an up and down, side to side movement. On flat areas, a chisel can be worked in as a wedge while wiggling the piece. When I get the piece apart, I lay the pile of pieces together in sections. Each section will be assembled first and then the sections will be put together for final assembly. You will find this 'compartmentalized' approach easier than assembling the entire piece all at once. For instance, I will glue the back of a chair and the front of the chair separately and then finish with the side rails. With a chest, I glue the end panels first and then the longer rails. For rocking chairs I glue the seat and base first, then do the upper back and arms. It is important to realize the reason for doing this is the glue grabs quickly and you need to clamp quickly to prevent a glue bond from forming in a position you don't want. If something does glue up wrong use white vinegar to soak the joints enough to take it apart again, which is why you need to use wood glue.

CHAPTER 3 - Cleaning and Preparation for Reassembly

The next step is to clean the old glue off the contact areas there are a number of ways to do this. The main goal is to remove glue, not wood. The flat areas and dowels can be cleaned using sand paper or files. Dremels with sanding drums and other bits are also great for this. Until you are sure of yourself go slow and be aware that you can chip the edges on the finished piece. (Fig. 2.) All dowel holes and mortise holes need to be cleaned using drill bits or a Dremel. Be careful not to enlarge the holes. Just remove glue. The next step is to make sure that any dowels remaining attached to parts are tight in their holes. If they are not, then using a pair of pliers, wiggle them loose and clean them along with their corresponding holes. (Fig. 3)

Figure 2 Using a file, (picture on left) and a Dremel with a sanding drum to clean old glue off.

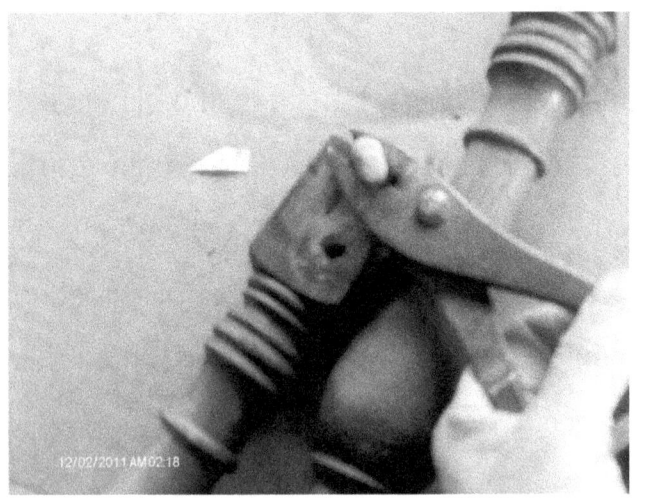

Figure 3 Checking dowel for tightness

CHAPTER 4 - Reassembly

I recommend dry fitting the pieces together first before applying glue to make sure you are getting it put back together correctly. There is nothing more discouraging than having to take a piece apart when glue has been applied. In dry fitting it is not necessary to fit every piece tightly back into place, just get familiar with where each piece goes in the assembly. Chairs in particular can be a trick due to the angles of legs into the seat, where stretchers meet legs.

Also while dry fitting, this is the time to start thinking about the clamping process. The clamping process is one of the most important parts of the reglueing procedure as it forces the glue into the pores of the wood and stabilizes the piece so that the glue bond is secure. It is very important to clamp all pieces tightly and pull all joints flush to where the manufacturer originally had them. Also bear in mind that there should be a barrier between the wood and the metal of the clamps (or ropes) otherwise you can dent and chip edges. I use rubber pads designed for my clamps, but I have also used thin wood or card board. Apply glue to all surface contact areas and in the dowel holes and proceed to put the pieces together again, making sure to clamp all parts tight. (Fig. 4) If for some reason a joint is not pulling together, take is back

Figure 4 Fully clamped chair, sitting on a level surface.

apart to see if the glue has been forced to the bottom of the dowel hole and is holding it apart. If so, use a tooth pick or whatever will fit into the hole and remove some of glue. Then use your pliers to squeeze a groove down the length of the dowel, this will allow the glue to move up the hole and not pocket at the bottom. Commercial dowels have ridges along them for this reason. Finally clean off any excess glue, set the piece on a flat level surface. A level may be used to ensure the piece is level. Usually adjusting the clamps can take care of leveling problems. In the appendix are pictures that demonstrate different clamping methods. If the dowel holes are larger than the dowels, I use a mixture of fine saw dust and glue to glue the parts together.(Fig 5.) If there is a big difference in the dowel holes and the dowels, then the existing dowels need to be replaced with larger dowels and the piece redrilled for the new dowel size. If screws won't tighten down when replacing them, use wooden tooth picks, glued in the holes and broken off at the same depth as the hole the screw hole is.There are additional pictures of clamping methods at the end of this text.

Now that I have made this all sound simple, life rarely goes that way and I do have answers for the problems as well, so stay calm and keep reading. Remember, its wood and I have found it can always be repaired or replaced.

Figure 5 Mixing glue and saw dust into a paste to be used in contact areas where there are gaps or looseness, dowel hole and mortise and tenon joints.

CHAPTER 5 - Broken Dowels

Broken dowels are probably the most common problem to deal with. The thing to keep in mind is that in cleaning out the old dowels to replace with new dowels, you do not want to enlarge the hole or change the original alignment of the dowel hole from the manufacturer's original direction.

First secure the piece with the broken dowel securely to the work area with a clamp and rasp the broken dowel flush with the surface using a file. Now you can mark the center area of the broken dowel. Use something sharp to make an indentation for a drill bit to sit in. Using a drill bit that is approximately half the size in diameter as the dowel, drill down into the center of the dowel until you feel the drill hit the pocket at the end of the hole. (Fig. 6) You can tell when this happens as the drill is not meeting the resistance of the wood. Then rotate the drill to enlarge hole that you are drilling, so that you leave a thin piece of the dowel in place. The other way is to simply increase your drill bit size until you leave a thin wall of the original dowel in place.

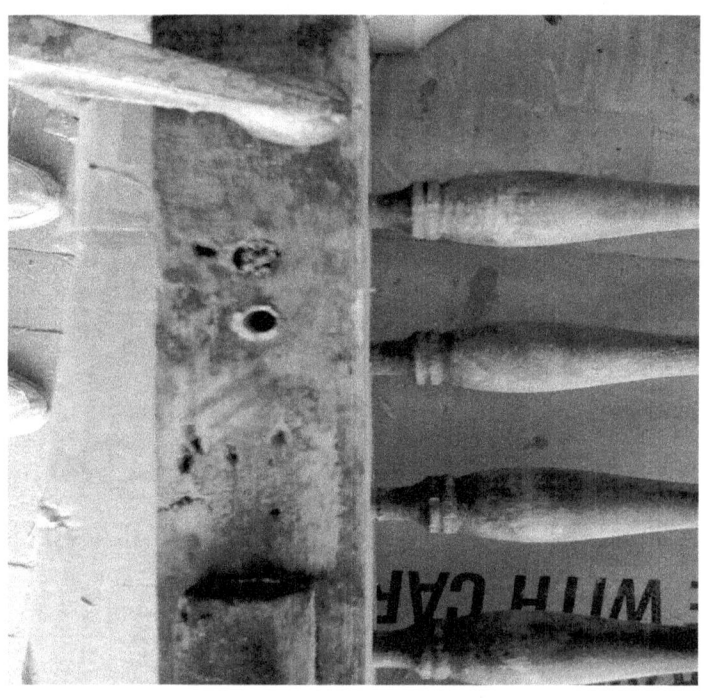

Figure 5 Piece securely clamped to work surface, with a hole smaller than the original dowel hole, drilled down the middle of the broken off dowel.

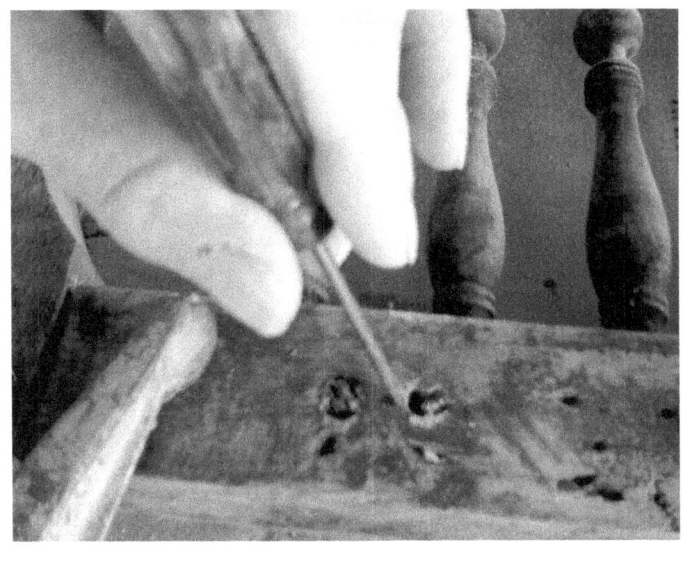
Figure 7 Cleaning out a dowel hole with a small flat head screw driver

Then use a small flat screw driver, place the flat end between the broken dowel and the wall of the dowel hole and carefully chip out the old dowel.(Fig. 7) Clean the hole out about a ¼ of an inch to verify the direction of the dowel hole. Using a drill bit the correct size for the dowel hole, finish drilling out the old dowel. Sometimes a broken dowel is loose in the hole, simply drill a pilot hole in the center of the dowel, screw in a screw to act as a handle and pull the broken dowel out. The size of the pilot hole is important. The screw as it is screwed in can cause the dowel to expand and become wedged in place.

CHAPTER 6 - Removing Nails and Screws

Nails can be tricky to find, as manufactures use nails to hold pieces together while the glue sets up and then putties over them. First dig out the putty with something sharp like and awl or ice pick. Then drill down with a small drill bit (1/8 or 3/16 in size) on two opposite sides of the nail head. (Fig. 8) Then use a pair of needle nose pliers to grab the nail head and gently lever the nail out. Be sure to put something under the pliers so as not to damage the wood. Many of the manufacturer's brads/nails are long so you may have to use the awl or ice pick in the drill holes to wiggle the nail loose. When you finally get the nail far enough out, you can use end cutters or diagonals to grab the nail and finish pulling is out. (Fig.9). If a nail breaks off, repeat the procedure or check to see it you got enough out to finish taking the piece apart.

Figure 8 Two small holes on either side of nail.

Figure 9. Pull the nail head out with Diagonals, note the wood piece between the chair part and the tool.

Screws can be difficult to remove for various reasons. Sometimes they are soft metal so the heads break off or the slots are wallowed out. A metal disk cutter on a Dremel tool can be used to cut a new slot (Fig. 10). Be cautious when you are using this method as it's easy to cut into the surrounding wood if this happens it will need to have putty applied later. Another way to remove stubborn screws is to create a slightly larger hole and drill the whole screw out. Screws that have rusted in place can be removed by drilling 3 or 4 small holes around the perimeter of the screw and then injecting WD40 into the holes. Allow the piece to soak overnight then cut a better slot in the screw. At that point you can insert the screwdriver in the newly cut slot and use a crescent wrench tightened onto the screwdriver to help rotate the screw out. (Fig. 11)

Figure 10 Cutting a deeper slot in screw head, if possible cut deep enough to cut into the screw shaft.

Figure 11 Crescent wrench allows for leverage on really tight screws.

Another method of screw removal is to tap on the screw head with a hammer and screw driver sometimes this is enough to move the screw in the wood and allow it to turn out. Occasionally just drilling off the head of the screw is enough to allow the pieces to come apart then you can finish turning the remaining screw out with vice grips.

Sometimes a screw that joins pieces together will break off if this happens a new hole will need to be drilled. The new hole should be angled as close to the same area as possible. There are pictures demonstrating most of these methods in the appendix.

CHAPTER 7 - Glue Injection

Sometimes a piece of furniture will have only one or two really loose joints and the rest are tight so a complete re-glue is not necessary. This method also works well on a piece of upholstered furniture where you don't want to remove a lot of material. The looser the piece the better this method works.

First you will need a 20cc syringe and a 14 gauge needle these can be purchased at a local feed and supply store.(Fig.12.) Start by cutting the flat pointed end off of the needle using an end cutter and then sand the end until smooth, proceed with caution as you can get a really nasty puncture wound. Next turn the piece over so that you are working from the underside. The idea is to create a very small hole in the rung to the already existing joint so that glue can be injected to the joint without pulling the two pieces apart.

Begin drilling with a 1/8 inch drill bit and angle it toward the joint you will know you've drilled as far as you need when you don't feel any resistance on the end of the bit. (Fig 13.) Sometimes a second hole is necessary to release the air in the pocket so the glue has some place to go. Now fill the syringe with wood glue and insert the needle and squeeze. (Fig. 14.) Try to get at least a ½ cc into the joint then use a tooth pick to plug the hole. If the parts will allow it, wiggle them a little to move the glue around.

Be careful when drilling not to twist the drill as small bits of wood can break off. If that happens just leave it in and start over. Clean off any glue and if there is a lot of movement to the joint, clamp the piece. Plug the hole with a tooth pick (Fig.15.).

I have also used screws under a piece as well to hold the joint. I don't like to do this as wood and metal expand and contract at different rates and that over time this will wear on the piece, hence you are removing wood from a joint area. The strength in the piece is from the complete structure of the wood.

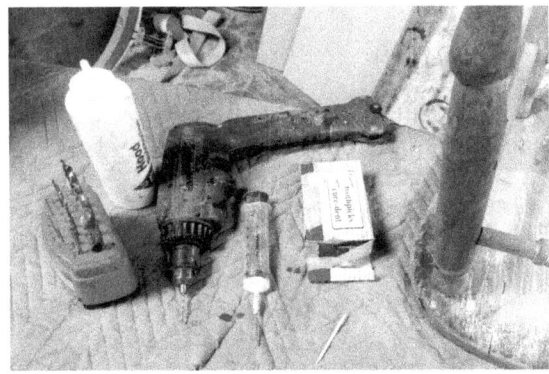

Syringe, Drill and glue, note the work is done from the bottom

Figure 13, Drill at an angle into joint

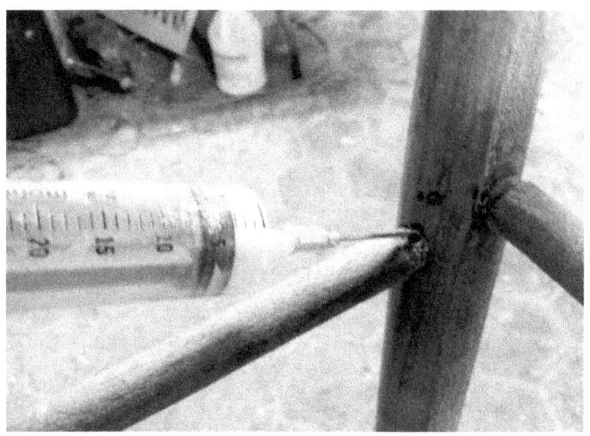

Figure 14, Injecting joint

Figure 15, Use a wood tooth pick to plug hole

CHAPTER 8 - Gluing Broken Parts

All broken wood can be glued. Furniture manufacturers regularly glue or laminate wood together to get pieces big enough for turned legs, solid wood table tops or wood panels. Many times pieces come apart simply because the glue has aged and dried out. In this case a piece can be repaired by simply sanding off the old glue, reapplying fresh glue

Figure 16 note the angled pieces in the broken wood.

and clamping the pieces back together. Breaks, whether long or short and jagged, should be coated thoroughly with glue and clamped tightly together. A dry run on clamping is important because sometimes once glue is applied it may allow the parts to slip so be sure parts are flush on all sides before you clamp. In gluing jagged pieces, make sure to remove any pieces that are not at the same angle as the direction of the grain of the wood as in (Fig.16).

Depending on the break sometimes it works best to slide the two pieces back together.

Figure 17, Sliding the piece into place with the direction of the wood grain.

This will lock the jagged ends together. Once again dry fitting is very helpful with this procedure. (Fig. 17) Short breaks should be reinforced after they've been glued, as the strength of the wood has been compromised. The main idea behind this repair is to cut a slot in the damaged piece of wood so that an undamaged piece can be inserted into the slot. The slot is often referred to as a mortise hole and the piece that is inserted into it is referred to as a tenon. I use two methods to do this. The first and easiest is a router with a slot cutter and bearing guide. I work from the underside of the piece wherever I can. When cutting out the mortise hole be careful to never remove more than ½ of the volume of the original piece and make the slot long enough so that it branches the break two to three inches on each side. Next you will need a new piece of wood that matches the color and grain of the damaged piece as closely as possible. You will use this to cut the tenon which will be placed in the mortise hole. Cut the tenon so that it will fit as tightly as possible and make sure you cut the piece along the

Figure 18 Holes drilled ready to clean out with a chisel

grain of the wood. Glue and clamp the new piece in, leaving some excess on the new piece to sand flush with the old. If a router cannot access the area, then mark a center line, down the piece as straight and accurate as possible. Drill holes along the line, (Fig. 18) again do not remove more than half the volume of the original piece wood. A one inch by one inch leg should have ½ inch holes, drilled a ½ inch deep.

Then clean the spaces between the holes out with a chisel making sure you have a clean even slot to position the new wood (Fig. 19.) Shape the new wood running the length of the grain on the piece and glue and clamp into place. Sand flush and finish. (Fig.20)

Figure 19 Tenon glued in place

Figure 20 Piece glued ready for sanding and finish

CHAPTER 9 - Repairing Broken Dowel Ends – Step Down Dowels

Many times a stretcher, rung or turned piece will break off at the very end leaving a part in the joining piece. These are fixed using a process called a step down dowel. (Fig. 21)First clean out the remaining broken dowel from the main piece by drilling it out using a smaller drill bit. The drill bit should be slightly smaller than the original dowel. This is the same method used to drill out a broken dowel.

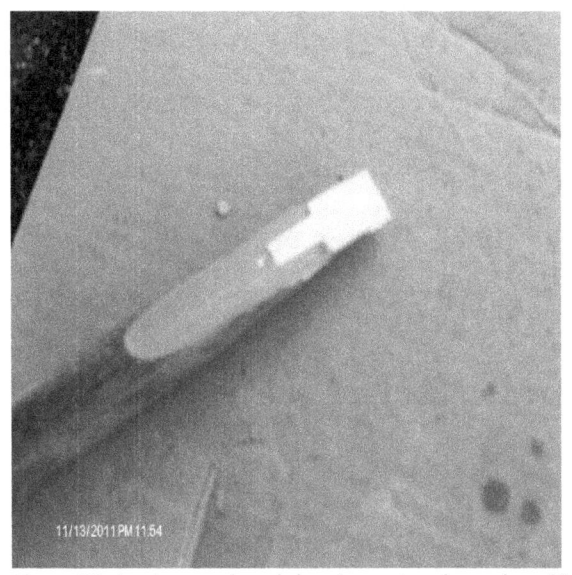

Figure 21 A cut away dowel showing a step down dowel in place

To continue with the repair you will need a dowel rod that is the same size as the end of the rung, stretcher or turned piece that you are repairing. If the exact size is not available then use the next largest size. Commercial dowel rods are available at most home improvement or hardware stores. I recommend oak or maple stock. Now take the broken piece and sand or file the end flat so that you can set a center point for drilling a hole. The hole should be no more than half the diameter of the piece being drilled and should be about 2 inches deep. Then using the new dowel rod, make a mark on it that is as far from the end of the rod as the depth of the hole that you're going to be placing it in. Then sand or file the rod down so that the dowel fits tightly in the new hole. (Fig. 22) Now you will need to fit the new dowel into the hole in the main piece of furniture. Measure the depth of the hole in the main piece of furniture where the new

Figure 22 The wood piece fits up into the hole and completes the back spindle.

dowel will be inserted. The dowel will need to be cut to a length that is just long enough to fit tightly in both holes but short enough so that the two pieces will fit flush together. I suggest that you dry fit the three parts together prior to applying glue to any of them. Once you have your new dowel fitting just right, remove it and use a pair of pliers to squeeze some shallow grooves down the length of it. This allows the glue to move along the piece providing a very effective seal. Glue the rung or turned end first then once it is well set, fit the newly repaired rung, stretcher or turned piece back into the main piece of furniture. There are more examples at the end of the text.

CHAPTER 10 - Replacing Missing Parts or Pieces

During the manufacturing of furniture many pieces such as legs, table bases or carvings are glued together first and then shaped, carved or turned to make the finished piece. After a period of time these pieces may dry out and come apart or the piece might be damaged or broken, resulting in damaged or missing pieces.

If none of the parts are missing, you can simply glue them back on. In most cases the parts will be flat on the joining sides and should be dry fitted to verify direction before applying glue. Sanding the flat areas first before applying the glue is a good idea. Be sure to only remove glue not wood and keep the surface area flat. After a light sanding, wipe the surface clean with a soft cloth and then apply a thin layer of glue and clamp the piece in place.

Occasionally there can be a problem with parts sliding or moving once glue has been applied this may require an alternative technique to clamping. One method is to tape the part in place, using masking tape. (Fig. 24) First hold the part in place applying gentle pressure for a minute or two, to give the glue a chance to bond. Then apply the tape over the area using as much pressure as the tape will bear without breaking.

Another method is to drill a pilot hole in the part being attached to the main piece. A pilot hole is a hole that is big enough to allow the screw to slide through the piece easily. Then hold the piece in place and drill another hole in the main piece using a drill bit smaller than the first, usually the size of the shaft of the screw being used. Then glue and screw into place tightly, but be careful not to tighten so as to split the wood. When the part is securely glued into place, remove the screw and putty the hole and touch up the part by sanding and applying the final color and finish.

When parts are completely missing there are various wood fillers, putties and epoxies that can be used to fill in the damaged areas, however, they may not always look right and they may not be a permanent solution. Many times these products can react adversely to temperature change and humidity by simply not bond correctly. Consequently, I prefer to repair this kind of damage using wood.

I begin by attempting to find a piece of wood that matches color, grain and species of wood as closely as possible. Once I've found a piece I can use for repairing, I create a flat area on the damaged piece so as to be able to attach the new piece of wood to the damaged area. Depending on the size of the damaged area, you can use a chisel, sanding paper, wood file or a combination of these to produce a flat surface area. The bigger and flatter the area, the stronger the glue bond to the new piece. (Fig. 23)

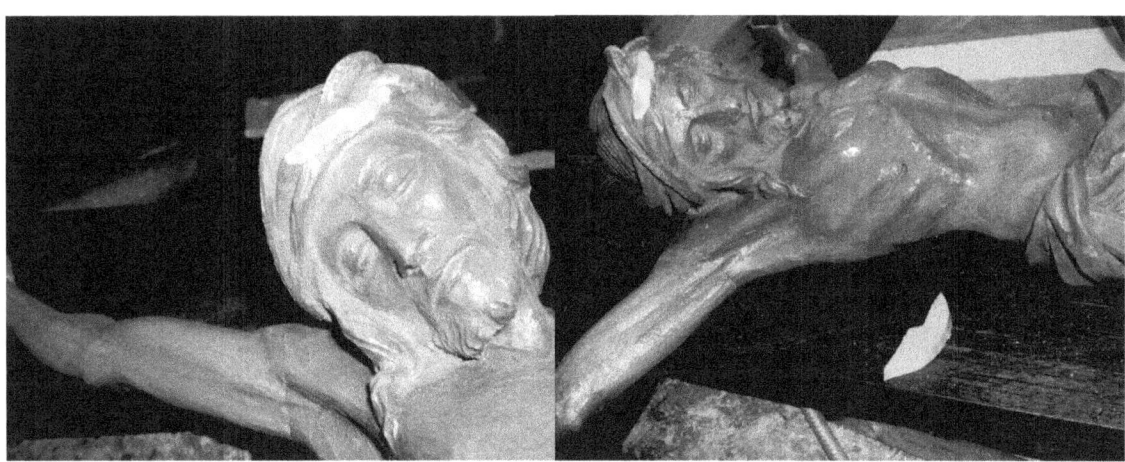

This piece broke during shipping.   Figure 23 The broken areas are filed flat, the new piece is cut.

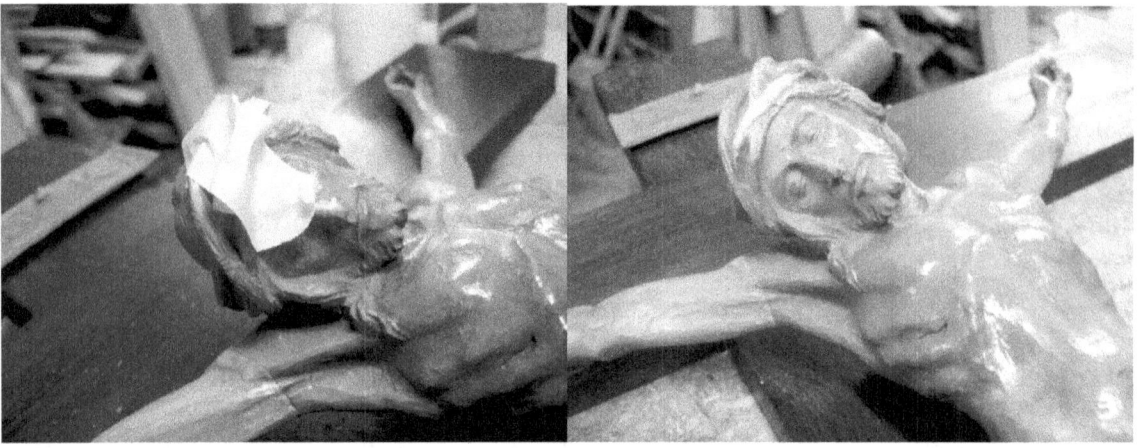

Figure 24 On irregular shapes masking taped hold parts until glue dries. Piece sanded into place, ready for touch up.

Next pre-shape the new piece of wood being added as closely as possible to the desired end shape, leaving it over sized. When you have rough shaped the new piece, glue it into place. When it is secure, then you can start to shape the new piece to fit and blend with the existing piece. I use my dremel with the sanding disk for this a lot, but wood files, sand paper, and chisels work also. I use the existing piece as a guide where the two pieces meet working my way out and around the new piece being fitted. Go slow and take time to study the part from different angles. When, the new piece is looking fitted, sand the final work into place feathering the new piece into the original part. Then apply the finishes required to blend the parts together. This is probably one of the most satisfying repairs I do, and if I take my time the end result is the piece is restored and doesn't look like anything ever happened to it.

CHAPTER 11 - Replacing or Repairing Veneer

To work with veneers you will need to add waxed paper, contact cement and flat pieces of wood or metal plate to your supplies. Contact cement is the standard in the industry for putting veneers down, however I have found that wood glue has enough moisture in it to make veneers pliable. Wood glue can help provide necessary moisture to work with old veneers that are warped or have sustained water damage.

If the veneer is chipped, split or lifted, but still in place, work glue under the edges with your finger until the glue comes out onto the surrounding area. Push the piece back into place, wipe off any excess glue. Place the wax paper over the area, cover with the flat piece of wood or metal and clamp tightly into place. I highly recommend wax paper for this application, but you may use plastic. If you do use plastic, be sure it is clear plastic without print or color as they can transfer to the veneer. Make sure everything is flat and there are no gaps around the wood or metal To repair bubbled veneer use a razor knife to cut a slit along the grain of the veneer, then using a syringe, inject glue into the bubble. (Fig. 25) Proceed to glue and clamp. (Fig. 26) I have used this method on table tops, cabinet sides, any place where the veneer has bubbled. When the glue is set and the clamps are removed, sand any raised areas flat and touch up.

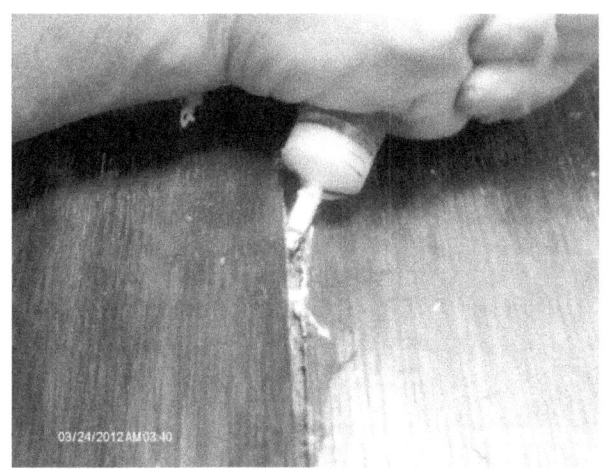

Figure 25 Injecting glue in cut area

Figure 26 Appling even pressure using long boards and clamps.

If pieces of veneer are missing there are various fillers and epoxies that can be used to fill in the missing areas on wood veneers, or missing areas can be filled with new wood.

First match as closely as possible the color of the wood and grain. Place a piece of paper over the area missing and do a pencil rubbing to gain a patterned image of the missing area. Cut out the pattern and mark it on the replacement veneer you have chosen. Check the paper pattern in the missing area for fit. Cut out the replacement piece using razor knife or scissors. Dry fit the two pieces together, if you are satisfied with the fit,

Figure 27 The missing veneer on the corner of the walnut chest has been filled in with walnut veneer and is ready for touch. At the end of the text are more step by step photos of this process.

then carefully sand a bevel edge around where the two pieces will meet. If there are some gaps, don't worry about them they can be filled later with filler. Apply wood glue to the original piece, only in the area where the veneer is missing, fit in the new piece, then glue and clamp tightly. When the glue is set, remove the clamps, sand the areas flush and proceed to touch up. If the area where the missing veneer is deeper than a single layer, cut several layers to fill in. With careful touch up this can be very successful. (Fig.27)

CHAPTER 12 - Tack Rails

Depending on how many times a piece has been upholstered, tack rails need to be repaired or replaced in order to give the fabric an area to be tacked to. Most of the time the rails can be filled, using a glue and saw dust mixture spread over the tacking area. Simply mix fine saw dust with wood glue into to paste, (Fig. 28) and work it into the damaged area. Allow the mixture to dry and proceed to reupholster the piece. The other method for tack rails is to make paper patterns of the shape of the rails, cut out new wood pieces for replacing the broken rails. Remove the broken rails by using a small saw, chisel or sand the areas flat, then glue and screw the replacement pieces in. (Fig. 29)

Figure 28 Glue and saw dust to fill in tack rail

Figure 29 New wood screwed into place.

CHAPTER 13 - Touch up of the finish

Figure 30 The original crack can be seen, but the area was sanded smooth and blended into the old finish. The dull color is the stain blended into the area. When the top coat is applied the area is shiny and not readily visible. When the stain is wet, that is what it will look like when top coated.

The first thing to keep in mind is safety and disposal of the products being used. Read all the manufactures labels and always work in areas with good ventilation. Wear gloves and protective clothing. This is the final stage to a good repair job and is probably the most important. If it is done right, the piece can look as if nothing has been done to it. In a standard reglue, many times the only thing necessary is simply wipe the piece down with a damp rag and make sure all the glue is off. If there are little chips, oils and polishes of the same color can be wiped on to cover these areas.

Sometimes more extensive work is needed in an area where you have glued pieces back together. Sand those areas down smooth and flush with 120 to 150 grit sand paper. Fill the holes with good wood putty. Occasionally a final sanding with 220 is necessary but try working with the lesser grit paper first. The reason for not using the fine grit paper is you can polish the wood so that it will not accept the stain and the finish will be lighter. Also when finish-sanding an area, you want to feather the area being sanded into the existing finish. (Fig. 30) This will let you blend in the stain. There are several self-sealing stains on the market and hard finishes that go over the top. Color is important as most wood finishes are all made up of four basic colors with variations added to them to get the final color. Walnut colors, Cherry, Oak, Maple etc., all are basic browns that are a green brown, a red brown or a yellow-brown. The basic tints for these colors are raw umber, burnt umber, raw sienna and burnt sienna, then reds, blacks, blues, greens and yellows can be added to get the hues needed. In some cases white is also added. If you cannot decide what color is predominant on the piece, hold something next to the piece that is a primary color, and you will see the color in the piece reflect the basic color. Then you can choose a stain that will allow you to blend the area in right. Most suppliers have color charts for free, that you can take home for reference.

When using commercial stains, it may take several coats applied over a period of time to achieve the depth of color necessary. Then when the stain is completely dry you will need a top coat. Most furniture has a lacquer top coat. There are spray lacquers on the market that are very good for going over the top and will allow you to blend in the finish. The first coat will feel rough, this is the sealing coat and when it is dry you need to lightly sand it smooth and reapply the top coat. Because spray finishes are lighter than brushed finishes, you may need to apply several coats. Also practice spraying on a piece of cardboard or wood first to get the feel for spraying. You want to avoid runs by just blasting away. Also be aware that there are several sheens available, but most furniture is usually gloss, semi-gloss or satin.

CHAPTER 14 - Do's and Don'ts

Don't take shortcuts unless you have previous experience. Much of what I do seems repetitive, but I found that rushing is usually when things go wrong. When I take my time, the job usually goes smoothly and I am more satisfied. I also build furniture and the things I have learned from my repairs have been very valuable to me.

As a general rule, glue the entire piece of furniture. This is particularly true for chairs. If some joints are not repaired they may become loose later making the repair more difficult as you will have some parts that are secure and these cannot be broken down again without possibly damaging the wood. The only caveat to this is if joint will not come apart without damaging the wood during the initial fix.

It is important to **always use wood glue.** Wood glue is designed to work with wood it has properties that allows it to have a certain amount of elasticity so that it will expand and contract with wood without losing its bond. If you have an overflow of glue to other surfaces it can be easily wiped off or sanded off. Epoxies, Super Glue, Gorilla Glue or other bonding agents are not designed to be used on wood. They may set up faster but the bond may not last and if you get it on surrounding areas they cannot be wiped off or sanded off without permanently damaging the finish on the piece.

Additional Photos for clamping

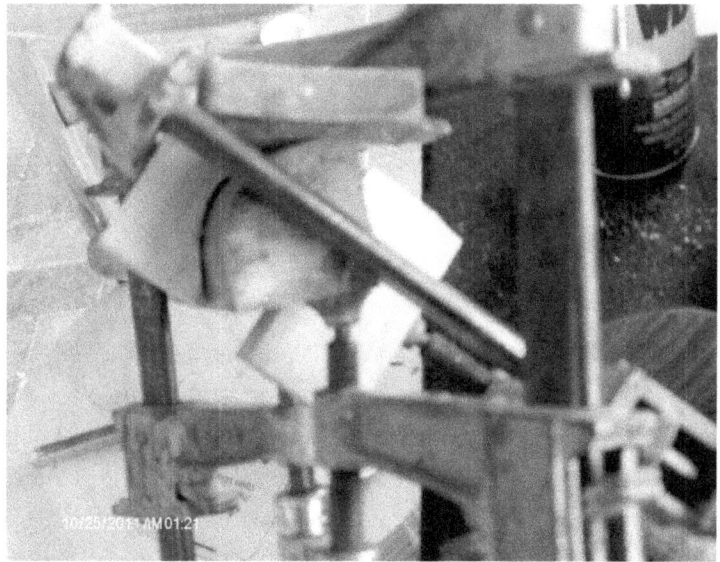

This chair leg was split down the middle. Note the pieces of wood cut out to the shape of the leg so that the clamps can apply direct pressure.

In order to clamp the split at the front of the rail, the straight piece of wood was clamped at the back first then at the front.

This piece is being glued in more than one direction. Notice the plastic between the board and the item being glued. It prevents the board from being glued to the piece as it is clamped into place to apply even pressure down the piece being glued.

This is a band clamp, a rope will work too. The rope can be tightened in the same way a tourniquet is applied in medical care. Cargo Straps could be used also.

ByCindy.co

Copy right Nov. 2012